EXPLORING
CAREERS

Careers in Business Administration

ReferencePoint
Press®

Other titles in the *Exploring Careers* series include:

EXPLORING CAREERS

Careers in Business Administration

Carla Mooney

ReferencePoint Press®

© 2018 ReferencePoint Press, Inc.
Printed in the United States

For more information, contact:
ReferencePoint Press, Inc.
PO Box 27779
San Diego, CA 92198
www.ReferencePointPress.com

LIBRARY OF CONGRESS CATALOGING-IN-PUBLICATION DATA

Name: Mooney, Carla, 1970– author.
Title: Careers in Business Administration/by Carla Mooney.
Description: San Diego, CA: ReferencePoint Press, Inc., [2018] | Series: Exploring Careers | Includes bibliographical references and index.
Identifiers: LCCN 2016059337 (print) | LCCN 2017010400 (ebook) | ISBN 9781682821923 (hardback) | ISBN 9781682821930 (eBook)
Subjects: LCSH: Management—Vocational guidance–Juvenile literature. | Business—Vocational guidance—Juvenile literature.
Classification: LCC HD38.2 .M66 2018 (print) | LCC HD38.2 (ebook) | DDC 658.0023--dc23
LC record available at https://lccn.loc.gov/2016059337

Contents

Working in Business Administration

A compliance officer at SouthPoint Bank in Birmingham, Alabama, Michele Durham works in one of the many careers in business administration. The laws, regulations, licensing, and permits that today's organizations must comply with has increased the need for officers like Durham, whose job involves making sure organizations follow internal policies and meet regulatory requirements. Compliance officers work in a broad range of industries, from health care to finance. Their responsibilities include evaluating the risks and regulations that affect an organization, setting up controls and procedures to make sure the organization follows rules and regulations, and monitoring and reporting on how effective these controls and procedures are.

For Durham, no day is the same. She arrives at work prepared to tackle a variety of projects, from training to regulatory reporting. In between, she solves employees' problems and answers questions about whether the organization is compliant with the latest rules and regulations. One of her biggest responsibilities is training bank staff to comply with all of the laws and regulations facing banks today.

To do her job, Durham must constantly stay on top of industry and regulatory news. When a new regulation is passed, she makes sure the bank's employees know what they need to do in order to be in lockstep with the law. For example, when new mortgage loan disclosure rules took effect in 2015, Durham prepared training materials for the bank's loan operations department and organized training sessions for the staff. "If I think there is something important out there . . . and I see training courses, I'm going to assign them," she said in a December 2015 article for *Independent Banker*.

Like many people in business administration, Durham helps keep her organization's day-to-day operations running smoothly. By managing these, she and other business administrators position an organization to implement long-term plans and meet its goals.

What Is Business Administration?

Every company, from the largest corporation to the tiniest start-up, needs skilled administrators if it is to succeed. Business administration is a wide career field that includes many types of management positions, from accounting and finance to marketing and operations. Business administration professionals work for companies in almost every industry, including health care, service, manufacturing, nonprofit, finance, technology, retail, government, and more. Regardless of industry or job function, business administration employees help a company manage its daily operations so it can reach its goals and objectives.

Business administrators can work in areas such as general management, hospitality management, office administration, operations management, retail management, and sales management. Some specialize in finance or technology. While job responsibilities vary by position, most business administrators develop and carry out department or company policies and procedures. In some positions, they oversee their department's budget and financial activities. Those who work in operations may oversee an organization's production department or departments that provide services. Business administrators often consult with other management and executive staff about improving an organization's operations and implementing new technologies. In some positions, they negotiate with customers and suppliers and approve contracts and agreements. They often spend time analyzing various business reports such as financial statements, sales reports, and performance reports.

Demand for Business Administrators

According to the Bureau of Labor Statistics, the demand for business administrators is expected to grow at approximately the average rate for all occupations between 2014 and 2024. While some business

Careers in Business Administration

Occupation	Minimal Education Requirements	2015 Median Pay
Administration service manager	Bachelor's degree	$86,110
Bookkeeper, accountant, auditing clerk	Some college, no degree	$37,250
Compensation and benefits manager	Bachelor's degree	$111,430
Economist	Master's degree	$99,180
Financial examiner	Bachelor's degree	$78,010
Human resources specialist	Bachelor's degree	$58,350
Insurance underwriter	Bachelor's degree	$65,040
Loan officer	Bachelor's degree	$63,430
Management analyst	Bachelor's degree	$81,320
Marketing manager	Bachelor's degree	$124,850
Market research analyst	Bachelor's degree	$62,150
Personal financial adviser	Bachelor's degree	$89,160
Sales manager	Bachelor's degree	$113,860
Administrative assistant	High school diploma or equivalent	$36,500
Financial clerk	High school diploma or equivalent	$37,040

Source: Bureau of Labor Statistics, *Occupational Outlook Handbook*, 2015. www.bls.gov.

administration careers require just a high school diploma or its equivalent, others require students to earn a bachelor's or master's degree from a four-year college or university. Students can major in business administration or a related field. Often, students take a wide variety of core business classes, such as management, marketing, finance, and accounting. In addition, many students concentrate in specific areas, such as human resources, finance, marketing, management, health services administration, and hospitality and tourism. Across all concentrations, a degree in business administration can provide a foundation of general business skills that can be used in a wide range of careers.

Administrative Services Manager

What Does an Administrative Services Manager Do?

At a Glance
Administrative Services Manager

Minimum Educational Requirements

Bachelor's degree; in some cases only a high school diploma

Personal Qualities

Strong leadership, communication, and problem-solving skills; attention to detail

Certification and Licensing

Not required, but can strengthen résumé

Working Conditions

Office environment, with some outside work

Salary Range

Median pay of $86,110 in 2015

Number of Jobs

As of 2014, about 287,300

Future Job Outlook

Projected growth of 8 percent through 2024

The more smoothly an organization runs, the more productive it will be. With this in mind, administrative services managers work behind the scenes to take care of a business's daily needs. They plan, direct, and coordinate the support activities that keep an organization running. Specific responsibilities vary by job and by organization. Most administrative services managers organize and maintain facilities, coordinate mail distribution, keep records, budget purchases, allocate supplies, and maintain the office environment. Smaller organizations may have one person—an office manager—who handles all of these tasks. Larger organizations may have several administrative managers who focus on a specific area or department.

A good administrative services manager can help an organization's employees be more productive and efficient. For example, he or she usually plans for and orders necessary supplies and services, such as paper and printer ink. He or she may also design an office floor plan and allocate space so that employees who work together sit near each other, which helps them be more efficient.

Administrative services managers can also save an organization money. Part of their job is to analyze a business's various costs, such as its energy consumption, technology use, and office equipment expenses. They use this information to recommend different paths of action, such as buying equipment that will lower energy costs or improve employee efficiency. They also plan for office equipment such as computers to be maintained or replaced. Replacing equipment at the right time can save an organization money, because it can often cost less to buy new equipment than to upgrade or maintain existing equipment.

Some administrative services managers specialize in certain areas. For example, facility managers oversee the operations and maintenance of an organization's building, grounds, equipment, and supplies.

The job of planning a company move, including which offices will go to which employees, often falls to an administrative services manager. These managers usually have a variety of duties, which involve planning and coordination of the activities that keep a business running smoothly.

They may supervise maintenance workers, security personnel, and groundskeepers. Facilities managers also help plan and manage projects that affect buildings, grounds, or other facilities. This includes renovating old buildings to bring them in line with governmental and environmental standards in order to make them use less energy, reduce waste, or better use their space. Facilities managers also work to make sure that facilities are safe, secure, and well maintained.

Other managers handle records. They create policies and procedures for keeping records, such as payroll records, customer invoices, or purchase receipts. They also make sure that company employees follow these procedures. They may arrange for records to be stored off-site or via an electronic content management system or database. Management will often ask a person in this position to pull records and provide critical information, such an employee's performance record or a customer's purchase history.

Katie Hively is an office manager for Artisan Talent, a staffing agency for creative, digital, and marketing jobs. In her role, Hively's work is always changing. "It would be easiest to say I assist with whatever the day brings!" she says in an interview posted on the Artisan website. "Whether that be greeting all of our amazing talent, or helping out with accounting, even just making sure everyone is set for the day." Hively likes that her colleagues can rely on her to take care of day-to-day tasks, help various departments that need it, and contribute to a positive work environment. She says the most rewarding part of her job is contributing to the entire company and helping things run smoothly. "I love being able to contribute to all branches within Artisan," she says. "The most rewarding part of my job is completing tasks that I know will make someone else's day just a little bit easier."

How Do You Become an Administrative Services Manager?

Education

Education requirements for this position vary from organization to organization. Most administrative services managers hold a bachelor's degree from a four-year college or university, although in some cases it is acceptable to have a high school diploma or its equivalent. Generally, students interested in becoming this kind of manager study business administration. Some take courses in engineering, public administration, facility management, or information management. Regardless of their degree, it can help to have some prior experience in a leadership or managerial position.

Certification and Licensing

Although this field has no required certifications or licenses, taking the initiative to become certified can improve a person's chance of landing a job. In particular, managers who specialize in facilities management or contract management often get certified in these areas. Professional organizations such as the International Facility Management Association and the National Contract Management Association offer several certifications that can strengthen a candidate's résumé. To earn these, a person must meet specific educational and experience requirements and may have to pass an exam.

Volunteer Work and Internships

Students interested in this career path can learn more by volunteering for local companies and organizations. Students can also learn more about a career in administrative services by interning with a local company or shadowing someone who already works in the field. In this way they can gain related work experience and learn the skills that will help them stand out to potential employers.

Skills and Personality

Successful administrative services managers need to be able to juggle many tasks at the same time. They also need solid problem-solving and communication skills. Administrative services managers usually oversee several staff members. This takes strong leadership skills—they must motivate their employees to do their best work. They must also diplomatically and fairly settle any disputes that arise between employees.

In this position, managers communicate with many people in their organization, from entry-level employees to executive management.

Therefore, an administrative manager must have strong communication skills. This includes the ability to speak clearly, listen to others, and write effectively.

It is also important for managers to have solid critical-thinking, problem-solving, and time-management skills and to pay attention to detail. Administrative services managers are often asked to identify problems in the organization and then develop and propose solutions. They frequently work on several projects at once and manage other employees' time. This means they must be very organized and efficient. At the same time, being able to wear many hats is critical for numerous tasks, from making sure that an organization meets building codes to managing the buying process for office supplies.

On the Job

Employers and Working Conditions

Every organization needs a good administrative services manager to keep it running smoothly. From nonprofit organizations to construction companies, administrative services managers work in virtually every industry. According to the Bureau of Labor Statistics (BLS), the industries that employed the most administrative services managers in 2014 were educational services (14 percent); health care and social assistance (13 percent); state and local government (11 percent); professional, scientific, and technical services (9 percent); and finance and insurance (8 percent).

Regardless of industry, administrative services managers spend most of their time working in an office. From time to time, they make site visits to inspect buildings and other facilities. They might also work outside to supervise groundskeeping and other facility maintenance.

Most administrative services managers work full time (forty hours per week). According to the BLS, about 25 percent work more than forty hours per week. Although they generally have defined work hours, administrative services managers must sometimes be on call during evenings and weekends to resolve any problems that occur after normal working hours.

Earnings

According to the BLS, as of May 2015 the median annual earnings for administrative services managers was $86,110. Wages ranged from less than $46,000 to more than $154,000. Administrative services managers typically receive other benefits too, which can be worth thousands of dollars. Benefits vary from employer to employer but usually include paid vacation and sick leave, bonuses, medical and dental insurance, education or tuition reimbursement benefits, retirement benefits, and life insurance.

Opportunities for Advancement

Managers who work for large organizations that employ multiple levels and types of administrative services personnel will have the best opportunities for advancement. Some managers transfer between departments or advance to positions that have more responsibility or supervise other positions. Others advance to higher-level positions, such as director of administrative services. Some experienced managers take jobs with management consulting firms, where they advise client organizations on how to make their offices more efficient.

When Christina Gregory first started working at Hope Plumbing in 2013, she helped the owners of that small business manage their day-to-day schedules and activities. As the Indiana company got bigger, Gregory proved herself a capable administrative services manager and was promoted to the company's director of operations. "As the company grew, I grew into this role," she said in a November 2015 interview with the *Indianapolis Star* newspaper. "Every business needs someone to assume the role of general manager. And as a company grows, there become layers of management." When asked about the job's potential for advancement, she said, "Just as I grew into this position as Hope Plumbing grew, I'll grow into the next job title as we continue to grow."

Managers who consistently demonstrate excellent performance and effective leadership are more likely to be promoted. Earning professional certifications or a master's degree in business administration or a related field can also improve a person's opportunities for advancement.

What Is the Future Outlook for Administrative Services Managers?

The job outlook for administrative services managers is good. According to the BLS's *Occupational Outlook Handbook*, employment of such managers is projected to grow 8 percent from 2014 to 2024. This rate of growth is about the same as the average growth rate for all occupations.

As more organizations consider the impacts their business has on the environment, there will be an ongoing or increasing need for facility managers to use energy wisely and reduce waste and costs. Facility managers will be needed to oversee projects that involve modifying buildings to meet current or changing environmental standards and regulations. At the same time, new technology and smart building features will provide facility managers with more detailed and timely information, such as alerts and maintenance reminders. However, it is important to note that while this information will help facility managers do their job, it may also reduce the number of managers needed.

Another driver of employment in this field is an increasing demand for records and information management. Managers who specialize in information governance, including privacy and legal issues, will be in high demand. As new technologies like cloud services transform how organizations store records, managers will be needed to help organizations implement them.

Because there are a limited number of higher-level positions, competition for these jobs is strong. Candidates who have work experience and can demonstrate a wide range of skills will have the best prospects for landing a job.

Find Out More

American Society of Administrative Professionals
website: www.asaporg.com

This organization provides online professional development, training, and other resources to address the changing role and demanding responsibilities of administrative professionals and executive assistants.

ARMA International

11880 College Blvd., Suite 450
Overland Park, KS 66210
website: www.arma.org

ARMA International is a not-for-profit professional association for individuals in records and information management. It publishes *Information Management* magazine, a journal for people who manage information as part of their job.

Institute of Certified Records Managers (ICRM)

230 Washington Ave. Ext., Suite 101
Albany, NY 12203
website: www.icrm.org

This organization is an international certifying body of and for professional records managers. The ICRM offers a six-part exam for professionals to earn the designation of certified records manager.

International Facility Management Association (IFMA)

800 Gessner Rd., Suite 900
Houston, TX 77024
website: www.ifma.org

The IFMA is the world's largest and most widely recognized international association for facility management professionals. It sponsors industry conferences and publishes materials for people working in facilities management.

General and Operations Manager

At a Glance
General and Operations Manager

Minimum Educational Requirements
Bachelor's degree

Personal Qualities
Strong leadership, communication, critical-thinking, and problem-solving skills

Certification and Licensing
Not required, but can strengthen résumé

Working Conditions
Office environment

Salary Range
Median pay of $97,730 in 2015

Number of Jobs
As of 2014, about 2,124,100

Future Job Outlook
Projected growth of 7 percent through 2024

Every organization has goals it wants to achieve, such as launching a new product, moving into a new facility, or achieving a certain level of profitability. General and operations managers help accomplish this. Their job is to plan, direct, and coordinate the operations of both private companies and public organizations so they successfully meet their goals. These managers create the strategies and policies that help an organization meet its goals and conduct operations. They work for private companies, nonprofit organizations, and government entities. Most of the time their responsibilities cross many departments and functional areas.

A large organization may have several levels of general and operations managers. Lower-level managers oversee day-to-day operations, while higher-level ones focus more on creating strategic plans

18

and developing policies. They may work with top executives such as chief executive officers (CEOs) and chief operating officers (COOs) to manage the company's overall direction. They may oversee the activities of one or more departments and make sure the organization is following the appropriate policies and procedures. General and operations managers often work closely with CEOs and COOs to ensure that the company's daily operations align with strategic goals.

General and operations managers' responsibilities can change depending on the type of organization for which they work. Their responsibilities also depend on the organization's size. Managers of a small organization might purchase inventory and supplies, hire and train employees, perform quality control to make sure products are up to company standards, and supervise the organization's day-to-day operations. They may also plan how materials and employees are used. Part of their job could be to schedule staff and assign work to make sure projects are completed accurately and on time. In larger companies, such managers might oversee activities when a company buys or merges with another company.

Some general and operations managers work for nonprofit organizations or local, city, state, or federal governments. Some of them are officials who are elected to office by voters. Others are city managers or county administrators who are appointed by government officials. Private and public school systems—from elementary to college—also employ general and operations managers. They oversee school operations and are involved in budgeting, resource planning, and general operations.

The operations manager of a major hotel in Louisiana says that much of his job involves supervising hotel staff to ensure guests have everything they need. "I spend the majority of my time supervising staff in different departments and making sure that everything is ready for guests to check in," he said in a 2015 *Lifehacker* interview. "I have to make sure my staff is happy because they are just as important as the guests. If you check in to a hotel with an unhappy staff, it shows." Therefore, he makes it a priority to make sure his staff members talk openly about any problems they are having. One way he does this is by holding daily meetings with all the managers and department heads. It is also his job to train staff so they all perform consistently and at a high level of quality. "I can't do all of this stuff by myself so I have to train all the employees to think like I think, as well as make sure they have all the tools they need to do their jobs."

How Do You Become a General and Operations Manager?

Education

The education required to be a general and operations manager depends on the industry and goals of each organization. Most managers have at least a bachelor's degree from a four-year college or university. They have likely concentrated in business administration, liberal arts, or a related area. Some managers, especially those who work as top executives in large companies, also have a master's degree in business administration or a related field. Generally, students interested in this career should take a broad array of business courses, including those in management, marketing, finance, and accounting. College presidents and school superintendents are usually required to have at least a master's degree, though a doctorate is preferred. For government positions there is no specific education requirement, but most administrators have at least a bachelor's degree.

In addition, most have a lot of related work experience. Some move up from lower-level positions in the same company. Others gain experience at other organizations and are hired into managerial positions. Candidates for senior positions need significant managerial and industry experience. For example, a person who applies to be a general and operations manager for a large sporting goods company should have prior work experience in retail.

Certification and Licensing

Although there are no required certifications or licenses for general and operations managers, some voluntary training and certifications can improve a person's chances of landing a job or getting promoted. Many organizations provide in-house instruction or pay for employees to attend third-party trainings or conferences. These programs can give employees a more detailed understanding of company operations and issues that impact the organization. "I did not need any licenses and certifications to get my job," says the Louisiana hotel manager, "but once you are a manager at a corporately-owned hotel, you have to go through at least three different training sessions per year on everything from hurricane procedures, fire procedures, health inspections, corporate responsibility, hotel standards, employee training, etc." Attending conferences and seminars can also help employees make important new contacts within an industry.

General and operations managers also attend local and national training programs to keep up with the latest trends in management. Managers who attend trainings sponsored by the Institute of Certified Professional Managers may be able to earn the Certified Manager credential. While this credential is not required to hold this kind of job, it demonstrates a person's command of good management skills.

Volunteer Work and Internships

Students interested in embarking on this career can learn about the field by volunteering for local companies, nonprofit organizations, and government entities. In this way students can gain related work experience and demonstrate leadership and managerial skills that will help them stand out.

Jayden Nelson, a student at Augustana University in Sioux Falls, South Dakota, worked as an intern for Sioux Falls Tower and Communications, a wireless communications company. During the internship, the general manager assigned Nelson various project manager tasks. "I was allowed to participate in weekly project manager meetings and help coordinate tasks for various jobs sites," he said in a 2015 interview published on the university's website. "Additionally, I was responsible for the creation of an AnchorGuard spreadsheet used to track the corrosion level on tower sites. This internship was easily one of the most valuable experiences in my college career."

Skills and Personality

General and operations managers need a range of skills and qualities to be successful. Strong leadership and managerial skills are critical. Consider that such managers usually oversee several departments and many employees. Therefore, they need strong leadership skills. They also need clear vision to make sure the organization meets its goals. In addition, as more companies operate globally, candidates who have international experience and foreign language skills will also be in demand.

General and operations managers also need to be effective and efficient communicators. They rely on their expert communication skills when they discuss issues with other executives, negotiate with customers and vendors, direct employees, and explain policies and procedures to those inside and outside the organization. All such managers require the ability to speak well, listen to others, and write clearly and effectively.

It also helps to have strong critical-thinking, problem-solving, and decision-making skills. General and operations managers are often asked to identify problems in the organization and develop and propose solutions. They need to be able to recognize where the organization is falling short of meeting its goals, assess different solutions, and choose the best one to get the organization back on track.

General and operations managers often juggle many tasks and projects at the same time. Therefore, it is extremely important to be able to effectively manage their time and their employees' time.

On the Job

Employers and Working Conditions

From nonprofit organizations to Fortune 500 companies, general and operations managers work in virtually every industry. According to the Bureau of Labor Statistics (BLS), there were about 2.1 million general and operations managers in 2014. They work in organizations that range in size from small businesses with a handful of employees to large corporations with thousands of workers.

Most such managers work in an office. They often put in long hours, including evenings and weekends. Many general and operations managers travel to other cities, states, and countries to visit a company's satellite offices or production facilities. They also travel to attend meetings and conferences.

This career can be stressful; there is often intense pressure to meet company goals such as reaching a certain profit level or keeping customers satisfied. General and operations managers and other top executives are usually held accountable for the organization's performance. If the organization does not meet its goals and expectation, its managers may be replaced.

Earnings

According to the BLS, as of May 2015 the median annual earnings for general and operations managers was $97,730. Because a general and operations manager's responsibilities vary widely by industry and organization, earnings also vary. In 2014 wages ranged from less than $44,190 to more than $187,200 for the highest-paid managers.

In addition, general and operations managers typically receive other benefits, which can amount to thousands of dollars. Benefits vary from employer to employer and can include paid vacation and sick leave, bonuses, medical and dental insurance, education benefits and tuition reimbursement, retirement benefits, and life insurance.

Opportunities for Advancement

General and operations managers who work for larger organizations will have the best opportunity for advancement. Some managers move between departments or advance to positions that have additional responsibilities and leadership roles. Others advance to higher-level positions, such as COO or CEO.

Experienced managers who demonstrate a record of excellent performance and effective leadership are more likely to be promoted. Company training programs and executive development programs can increase their likelihood of being promoted. Earning professional certifications or a master's degree in business administration or a related field can also help.

What Is the Future Outlook for General and Operations Managers?

The job outlook for general and operations managers is good. Top executives, including general and operations managers, are needed in all industries. According to the BLS's *Occupational Outlook Handbook*, employment of general and operations managers is projected to grow 7 percent from 2014 to 2024. This rate of growth is about the same as the average for all occupations. Job growth will vary by industry and will depend on how much the industry grows.

One of the main drivers of growth for this career is the formation of new organizations and the growth of existing ones. As new companies form, they will need experienced executives to run them. General and operations managers who have significant work experience and a proven record of success will be in high demand. However, if new companies are not being formed very quickly or corporate growth slows, this could negatively affect the demand for general and operations managers.

General and operations managers typically face strong competition for jobs. Although education requirements vary by industry, candidates who have strong leadership skills and impressive work experience will have the best job prospects.

Find Out More

American Management Association
website: www.amanet.org

The American Management Association provides a variety of educational and management development services to businesses, government agencies, and individuals.

Financial Management Association International (FMA)
University of South Florida
College of Business Administration
4202 E. Fowler Ave., BSN 3416
Tampa, FL 33620
website: www.fma.org

The FMA provides information about financial decision making, publishes research on important financial issues, and hosts annual finance conferences. These resources can be useful for general and operations managers who want to sharpen their finance and budgeting skills.

Institute of Certified Professional Managers

James Madison University
MSC 5504
Harrisonburg, VA 22807
website: www.icpm.biz

This is the largest management certifying body in the United States. It offers several certification programs.

National Management Association (NMA)

2210 Arbor Blvd.
Dayton, OH 45439
website: https://nma1.org

The NMA is a professional association dedicated to developing leadership and management skills. It offers certification and continuing education units to members.

Executive Assistant

What Does an Executive Assistant Do?

An executive assistant provides high-level administrative support to a company's executives. Like a secretary or administrative assistant, executive assistants perform clerical tasks needed to run an organization efficiently. They answer and make phone calls, coordinate meetings, make travel reservations, type and send memos, receive visitors, review reports, and manage an executive's daily schedule. They use computers to create spreadsheets and manage databases. They prepare presentations, reports, and documents. Some executive assistants work with vendors to buy supplies. Others manage company stockrooms and libraries. They also use a variety of office equipment, including computers, videoconferencing equipment, and fax machines.

Today's executive assistants are more than just clerical workers, however, and often take on added responsibilities. Many are involved in project management and strategic planning, and they often work directly with

---

At a Glance

Executive Assistant

Minimum Educational Requirements

High school diploma or equivalent

Personal Qualities

Strong communication; organizational, time management, and interpersonal skills

Certification and Licensing

Not required, but can strengthen résumé

Working Conditions

Office environment

Salary Range

Median pay of $53,370 in 2015

Number of Jobs

As of 2014, about 776,600

Future Job Outlook

Projected decline of 6 percent through 2024

executives. "The executive assistant role used to be pretty singular. It was a support role, and the [executive assistant's] primary job was following orders," said Emily Allen, director of programs and services at the International Association of Administrative Professionals in a November 2014 interview on the Brazen Technologies website. "Now, the executive assistant is being brought in on decision-making processes. Executive assistants are being put in charge of whole projects." In addition, they may analyze documents, conduct market research, and prepare statistical reports for executives.

When executives face numerous demands on their time and attention, the executive assistant often acts as a gatekeeper, controlling phone calls and reports that go to the executive. The executive assistant also manages the executive's schedule and controls which meetings are placed on his or her calendar.

Depending on the organization's size, executive assistants may lead a team of assistants and clerical workers. Some work closely with

An executive assistant provides high-level administrative support to a company's executives. This might include clerical tasks as well as preparing and reviewing reports, creating spreadsheets, managing databases and stockrooms, and more.

lower-level administrative assistants. Often, executive assistants co-ordinate the workload and assignments among the staff. They also train incoming assistants on the company's needs.

Executive assistants must be flexible and prepared to handle any assignment that comes their way. "Very often things change over-night or in the morning," says Stacy Leitner in a *U.S. News & World Report* article. Leitner is an executive assistant to the city manager of Rancho Cordova in California. "You have to be willing to handle confrontation, be a hard worker and be professional while flexing to the individuals you work for." Leitner's day starts with a list of tasks, which are often rearranged when something with a higher priority arises. "It's very fast-paced," she says.

A good executive assistant can become an indispensable part of a company. "You'll recognize the amount of influence you have on deci-sions. You have the ability to speak up, and you are the CEO's confi-dant," says Leitner. "You are exposed to confidential information be-fore it's implemented, and you can provide input, interject ideas and provide a different perspective."

How Do You Become an Executive Assistant?

Education

Most executive assistants have at least a high school diploma. Al-though a college degree is not required, taking business courses and earning an associate's or bachelor's degree in business administration or a related field can give one an advantage over the competition. Some employers prefer to hire an executive assistant who has a college degree or who has taken college-level business courses. High school graduates can take technical school or community college courses in word processing, spreadsheet software, database software, and office procedures.

In addition, many executive assistants benefit from on-the-job training. Over a few weeks to months, they learn an organization's administrative procedures and their specific responsibilities. This training period helps them become familiar with any industry-specific terminology and procedures.

Many executive assistants have several years of work experience in a related occupation. They may have been a secretary or a lower-level administrative assistant within the same organization or a different one. After learning the basics, they moved up to executive assistant positions, where they have more challenging responsibilities.

Certification and Licensing

Although executive assistants do not need any certifications or licenses, getting certified can improve their chance of landing a job or can increase their paycheck. Getting certified shows a person is committed to his or her career and to continued learning. "You need to be a lifelong learner," says Leitner. "Certifications help you to develop and embrace technology."

Professional organizations such as the International Association of Administrative Professionals offer several certifications that can strengthen a candidate's résumé. To earn these, candidates must have a certain level of education and experience and may have to pass an exam.

Volunteer Work and Internships

Students interested in this career can learn more by volunteering or interning for a company or nonprofit organization. In this way students can gain related work experience and stand out to potential employers.

Jaimee Erickson interned at a medical center while going to school to be an executive assistant. In an interview published on Wisconsin Indianhead Technical College's website, she says, "The internship has been a great way to apply the skills I have learned. It has also allowed me to gain real-life experience in workplace situations." She recommends that all students try an internship. "An internship is a good way to see if your area of study is right for you, and to see if you will enjoy the work you are getting into."

Skills and Personality

Successful executive assistants have several skills and qualities that allow them to advance within the field. In this position, a person must communicate and interact with many people, including employees, clients, and executive management. Therefore, he or she should have strong communication and interpersonal skills. The ability to speak well, listen to others, and write effectively will also facilitate good communication. A strong command of grammar can help, as executive assistants will likely be responsible for writing memos and other communications. Their interactions with others should contribute to a positive work environment and client experience.

Attention to detail, time management, and organizational skills are also critical for success. Executive assistants must handle many tasks at the same time, making sure that every detail is planned. They keep files, folders, and schedules in order so executives can run an organization efficiently. In addition, executive assistants often handle sensitive information regarding an organization's strategies, employees, and customers. They must handle this information with integrity and make sure it is kept confidential.

On the Job

Employers and Working Conditions

A good executive assistant helps keep an executive team running smoothly. Executive assistants work in virtually every industry, from nonprofits to accounting. According to the Bureau of Labor Statistics (BLS), there were approximately 776,600 executive assistants working in 2014.

Regardless of industry, most executive assistants spend most of their time working in an office. Some telecommute or work from home as virtual assistants. Most work full time, or forty hours per week, typically during defined hours.

Earnings

According to the BLS, the median annual earnings for executive assistants was $53,370 as of May 2015. They also tend to receive other benefits, which can amount to thousands of dollars. Benefits vary from employer to employer and can include paid vacation and sick leave, bonuses, medical and dental insurance, education benefits, retirement benefits, and life insurance. "There are amazing possibilities in this profession," says Leitner. "You can make minimum wage or seven figures. You can work in any industry—in government, education, retail, hospitality and recreation. With the right skill set and industry, it can be very lucrative."

Opportunities for Advancement

Executive assistants who work for large organizations that employ multiple levels and types of administrative and executive assistants will have the best opportunity for advancement. Some executive assistants transfer between departments or advance to positions that have more responsibility. Others move into higher-level positions, such as office supervisor or manager.

Experienced executive assistants who demonstrate a record of excellent performance are more likely to be promoted. Earning professional certifications or an associate's or bachelor's degree in business administration or a related field can also improve a person's opportunities for advancement.

What Is the Future Outlook for Executive Assistants?

According to the BLS's *Occupational Outlook Handbook*, executive assistant positions are projected to decline 6 percent from 2014 to 2024. However, this job is in the midst of change that could bring new opportunities in the future. While technology has made it easier to perform clerical tasks previously done by executive assistants, executives are increasingly relying on them to manage projects and analyze company data and reports.

Because there are a limited number of higher-level executive assistant positions, competition for these jobs is expected to be strong. Candidates who have work experience and can demonstrate a wide range of skills will have the best prospects for landing a good job in this area.

Find Out More

American Society of Administrative Professionals
website: www.asaporg.com

The American Society of Administrative Professionals provides online professional development, training, and resources to address the changing roles and responsibilities of executive assistants.

Association of Executive and Administrative Professionals
900 S. Washington St., Suite G-13
Falls Church, VA 22046
website: www.theaeap.com

This association offers its members networking opportunities, education, seminars, a newsletter, and other information about what a career as an executive and administrative professional is like.

International Association of Administrative Professionals
10502 N. Ambassador Dr., Suite 100
Kansas City, MO 64153
website: www.iaap-hq.org

This association provides information, education, and certification for individuals who work in office and administrative professions.

International Virtual Assistants Association
3773 Howard Hughes Pkwy., Suite 500S
Las Vegas, NV 89169
website: http://ivaa.org

The International Virtual Assistants Association provides continuing education, networking opportunities, and information for people who want to become a virtual assistant or use their services.

Human Resources Specialist

At a Glance

Human Resources Specialist

Minimum Educational Requirements

Bachelor's degree

Personal Qualities

Strong communication and interpersonal skills; attention to detail

Certification and Licensing

Not required, but can strengthen résumé

Working Conditions

Office environment

Salary Range

Median pay of $58,350 in 2015

Number of Jobs

As of 2014, about 482,000

Future Job Outlook

Projected growth of 5 percent through 2024

Every company needs a human resources (HR) department to manage its employees. HR specialists focus on recruiting people to come work for the company. They are also responsible for placing new hires in the correct position. These professionals may also handle compensation and benefits, training and development, and employee assistance programs that help employees deal with problems that affect their work. "Human resources jobs may literally involve any aspect of an employer's workforce," says Nancy H. Segal, owner of an HR consulting firm called Solutions for the Workplace. In an article for *U.S. News & World Report*, she says, "There's enough variety for everyone, and each specialty requires a different knowledge base."

HR specialists often screen potential employees, conduct interviews, and perform background checks. When a new employee is hired, they welcome the person to the organization and give them an orientation. They often help administer employee benefits such as health insurance, retirement plans, and vacation days. They are typically tasked with processing payroll and help make sure the organization is in compliance with any local, state, or federal regulations. They also tend to be involved in employee relations, training, and annual review processes. In addition, HR specialists often oversee employees' satisfaction with their job and the workplace. They guide employees through all procedures and answer questions about policies. Above

A human resources specialist discusses company benefits with a newly hired employee. Individuals who do this job have to be knowledgeable about a company's health insurance, retirement plan, and vacation policy, among other things.

all, an HR specialist serves as a link between the organization and the employee. Their general responsibility is to make sure that the organization finds, hires, retains, and develops the best employees it can.

Heather Clark is the HR director at the Huntzinger Management Group. She started as an intern and was promoted to administrator, then manager, and she currently serves as director. Clark described her job in a June 2014 interview on the AfterCollege website. "It may come as a surprise, but, there is no typical day!" she said. "Every day is different and every day means a new challenge in my world." Clark said HR specialists must be able to prioritize the many—and sometimes unpredictable—tasks a day may bring. "The employee who can't log in to your online [HR] system because they forgot their password six times can wait when you have an upset client because of employee misconduct. Payroll goes wrong? Take that right to the top of your list. There is nothing that will upset your employees more than an inconsistent and incorrect paycheck." One of her favorite parts of the job is being able to help her coworkers. "When I can satisfy my superiors and my employees, it is a job well done," she said. "Nothing is more gratifying. Whether it's solving a health insurance issue for them, rolling out a new benefit, or simply helping them get through the day."

How Do You Become an HR Specialist?

Education

Most HR specialists have at least a bachelor's degree in HR, business administration, or a related field. It is helpful to take courses in business, industrial relations, psychology, writing, HR management, and accounting. Some organizations require previous work experience, which can be gained by working as an HR assistant, doing customer service, or serving in a related job.

Some HR specialists who wish to advance to a higher level earn a master's degree in HR. They can specialize in areas such as HR management, organizational development, and HR performance. Some HR specialists choose to pursue a master of business administration in HR management. Earning a graduate degree may help them get promoted or land a better-paying, more senior position.

Regardless of industry, HR specialists spend most of their time working in an office. Some travel to attend job fairs, visit college campuses, or meet with job applicants. Most work full time, or forty hours per week, typically during defined hours. Some positions feature flexible hours and telecommuting.

Earnings

According to the BLS, as of May 2015 the median annual earnings for HR specialists was $58,350. The lowest 10 percent earned less than $34,120, while the highest 10 percent earned more than $99,920. HR specialists typically receive other benefits too, which can amount to thousands of dollars. Benefits vary from employer to employer and often include paid vacation and sick leave, bonuses, medical and dental insurance, education and tuition reimbursement benefits, retirement benefits, and life insurance.

Opportunities for Advancement

HR specialists who work for large organizations that employ multiple levels and types of HR professionals will have the best opportunity for advancement. Some advance to positions that have more responsibility and may supervise others. Some advance to even higher positions such as HR manager or director.

HR specialists are likely to be promoted if they demonstrate a thorough knowledge of their organization, its needs, and its regulatory requirements. Earning voluntary professional certifications or a master's degree in business administration or a related field can also improve a person's opportunities for advancement.

What Is the Future Outlook for HR Specialists?

According to the BLS's *Occupational Outlook Handbook*, HR specialist jobs are projected to increase 5 percent from 2014 to 2024. This growth is being driven by an increase in employment services firms such as placement agencies, temporary help services, and professional employer organizations. As more companies outsource their

HR functions, job opportunities at these types of firms are expected to increase. In addition, as experienced HR specialists retire and leave the workforce, companies will need to replace them. HR specialists who have general skills and are able to handle increasingly complex employment laws and health care options will be in demand.

At the same time, the increasing use of technology is expected to slow the rate of growth in this field. As more employers use the Internet to recruit new employees and conduct other administrative tasks, they will need fewer HR employees to process employee records and information. Overall, though, job prospects for HR specialists are expected to be good. Candidates who have a bachelor's degree, voluntary certifications, and related work experience will have the best prospects for landing a job in the field.

Find Out More

HR Certification Institute (HRCI)
1725 Duke St., Suite 700
Alexandria, VA 22314
website: www.hrci.org

The HRCI is a credentialing organization for HR professionals. Its site has information about a variety of HR certifications.

National Human Resources Association
PO Box 16802
Rochester, NY 14616
website: www.humanresources.org

The National Human Resources Association offers professional networking forums, development tools, conferences, seminars, on-demand webcasts, and audiocast events.

Society for Human Resource Management
website: www.shrm.org

The world's largest society for HR professionals offers information and tools about a variety of HR topics, including certification, training, and career tracks.

WorldatWork
14040 N. Northsight Blvd.
Scottsdale, AZ 85260
website: www.worldatwork.org

This organization is a nonprofit HR association for professionals and organizations focused on compensation, benefits, work-life effectiveness, and total rewards. Its website has industry resources, information about education and certification, events, and more.

Management Analyst

What Does a Management Analyst Do?

Management analysts find ways to improve an organization's operations, make it more efficient, and increase its profits. Organizations of all sizes hire management analysts, who are also sometimes called management consultants. Management analysts talk to people at every level in an organization, from frontline employees to company executives. They interview an organization's vendors (companies that provide it with goods and services) and clients. They collect and analyze data about how a company works and determine its strengths and weaknesses. Using this information, they recommend ways to improve operations, decrease costs, increase efficiency, and grow revenues. "We want to help make the client better at what they do," says Mel Wolfgang, a senior partner at the Boston Consulting Group, a management consulting firm. In an article for *U.S. News & World*

At a Glance
Management Analyst

Minimum Educational Requirements
Bachelor's degree

Personal Qualities
Strong communication, interpersonal, analytical, and problem-solving skills; attention to detail

Certification and Licensing
Not required, but can strengthen résumé

Working Conditions
Office environment

Salary Range
Median pay of $81,320 in 2015

Number of Jobs
As of 2014, about 758,000

Future Job Outlook
Projected increase of 14 percent through 2024

Report, Wolfgang says, "Part of giving great advice to clients is looking at their challenges with a really fresh perspective. You need to be really intellectually curious to think through these tough problems from many different angles."

In a typical day, management analysts work to solve a problem or improve a process. They research and gather information about the problem. This might include interviewing company employees and visiting facilities to observe operations, equipment, and existing procedures. Management analysts also gather financial reports and other data regarding their project. They analyze the information and compare company procedures with those of similar companies. Then they come up with a solution or make recommendations to improve a process. Typically, management analysts write up their recommendations in a report and also prepare a presentation for senior management. After the organization makes the changes, management analysts meet with managers to make sure the expected results are being achieved.

While some management analysts work directly for an organization, others work for consulting firms or as independent consultants. Organizations hire consultants on a contract basis for specific projects. "Consulting works best for people who like to learn by doing, who like to do a variety of different things and who like solving problems," says Peter Aman, managing partner at the consulting firm Bain & Company. In an article in *U.S. News & World Report*, he says that consultants need to be able to jump from project to project. "You have to make sure you have the personality suited for an ever-changing environment," he says. "Not everybody wants that sort of constant change."

Whether they work for an organization, work for a consulting company, or are self-employed, the work of management analysts varies with each project. Some projects use a team of analysts who work together. On other projects the analyst may work alone. A project may focus on any part of an organization's operations, from its manufacturing processes to its accounts payable department. Some management analysts specialize in certain areas, such as managing inventory or streamlining an organization's structure. Others specialize in specific industries, such as technology or health care.

How Do You Become a Management Analyst?

Education

Most management analysts have at least a bachelor's degree from a four-year college or university. They typically major in business administration or a related field. To advance in the field, many also obtain a master's degree in business administration. When pursuing these degrees, students should take classes in a range of subject areas, including business, management, economics, political science and government, accounting, finance, marketing, psychology, and computer and information science.

Many analysts also have several years of related work experience in fields such as management, human resources, and information technology. Organizations typically prefer candidates who have experience in a particular industry or who specialize in the focus of the client's project. This experience helps analysts solve problems and make informed and effective recommendations.

Certification and Licensing

Although management analysts do not need to be specially certified or licensed, they can choose to take additional training or get certified. Doing so can improve a person's chances of landing a job or getting promoted. Certain professional organizations offer several types of certification. For example, the Institute of Management Consultants USA offers the Certified Management Consultant certificate. To earn this, candidates must meet minimum levels of education and experience, submit client reviews, and pass an interview and an exam. Once certified, management analysts must be recertified every three years.

Management analysts also attend local and national conferences to stay on top of latest trends in the industry. Attending such conferences can show a person's commitment to acquiring new knowledge and skills.

Volunteer Work and Internships

Students interested in a career as a management analyst can learn about this field by volunteering for local companies, nonprofit organizations, and government entities. In this way students can gain related work experience and demonstrate leadership and managerial skills that will help them stand out to potential employers. Brittany Webb worked for two summers as an intern for Northrop Grumman Corporation while she was an accounting student at Morgan State University. Webb worked as a business management analyst. Some of her responsibilities included extracting data from company databases, updating weekly reports, and preparing files and data for upcoming contract proposals. She also attended several events for company interns.

Skills and Personality

Successful management analysts must possess certain skills and qualities if they are to advance. For example, management analysts spend much of their time working with others, including people of all different backgrounds; having strong interpersonal skills makes this easier.

In addition, successful management analysts have solid mathematical, analytical, and problem-solving skills. They spend much of their time gathering a wide range of data about an organization. They must be able to quickly analyze this information if they are to propose realistic solutions and make useful recommendations. Because every client and problem is different, the analyst must be able to think creatively. Recommendations should fit each client's needs and goals. "You need to know how organizations work and how companies work, and you have to like solving problems and fixing things," says Aman. "You need to have a sharp analytical mind and the ability to establish frameworks and analyze things in an efficient manner."

Management analysts must also be able to write and speak well and to listen to others. They also often work under tight deadlines. Therefore, it is very important to be able to effectively manage their time and meet deadlines.

On the Job

Employers and Working Conditions

Management analysts work in many industries. While some work directly for large organizations, many work for consulting firms that contract with other companies on special projects. Others are self-employed and contract with companies directly on a project-by-project basis. According to the Bureau of Labor Statistics (BLS), there were approximately 758,000 management analysts working in 2014. The areas that employed the most management analysts were management, scientific, and technical consulting services (22 percent); finance and insurance (10 percent); the federal government (8 percent); and state and local governments (7 percent).

Management analysts split their time between their offices and client sites. They spend a lot of time with clients, which can require frequent travel. This career can be stressful. In order to meet tight deadlines, management analysts often work more than forty hours per week.

According to the BLS, in 2014 about 20 percent of management analysts were self-employed. Self-employed analysts have more control over their schedule. They can decide how many projects to take on and what travel they are willing (or unwilling) to do. However, because they only earn money when working on a project, self-employed management analysts must devote time to selling their services and expanding their client base.

Earnings

According to the BLS, as of May 2015 the median annual earnings for management analysts was $81,320. In 2014 wages ranged from less than $45,970 to more than $150,220 for the highest-paid managers. Management analysts who work for a consulting company usually receive a base salary plus an annual bonus. Analysts who are self-employed are paid either by the hour or by the project.

In addition, management analysts who work for an organization or consulting firm typically receive other benefits, which can amount to thousands of dollars. Benefits vary from employer to employer. These can include paid vacation and sick leave, bonuses, medical and dental insurance, education benefits and tuition reimbursement, retirement benefits, and life insurance.

Opportunities for Advancement

Experienced management analysts generally have the opportunity to take on more-complex projects. Senior-level analysts may supervise teams of analysts who are working on a large project. They may also focus on getting new clients and selling new projects to existing clients. Some analysts who work for a consulting firm may advance to higher-level positions and may even become a partner in the firm and share in its profits. Other senior analysts may leave a consulting company to take a senior management role at a client company.

Experienced management analysts who demonstrate a record of excellent performance are more likely to be promoted. Earning professional certifications or a master's degree in business administration or a related field can also improve a person's opportunities for advancement.

What Is the Future Outlook for Management Analysts?

The job outlook for management analysts is very good. According to the BLS's *Occupational Outlook Handbook*, employment of management analysts is projected to grow 14 percent from 2014 to 2024. This rate of growth is much faster than the average for all other occupations.

To stay competitive, many companies are looking for ways to become more efficient and control costs. As a result, the demand for management analysts is expected to increase across several industries. One is health care. As the population ages, health care companies are facing higher costs. In addition, federal health care reform is putting more pressure on health care providers and insurance companies to become more efficient and less expensive. Management analysts will be needed to recommend ways to address these issues. Government agencies are also looking to reduce spending and increase efficiency, so they too will be in need of management analysts. As US companies expand their businesses overseas, they are expected to need more management analysts to help them develop strategies for conducting business in foreign countries.

Management analysts are often well paid. This makes these positions highly desirable. Therefore, candidates face strong competition for open positions. Those who have a graduate degree, special certification or related work experience, are fluent in a foreign language, or are good at selling projects and bringing in clients will have the best prospects for landing a job in the field.

Find Out More

American Management Association
website: www.amanet.org

The American Management Association provides a variety of educational and management-development services to businesses, government agencies, and individuals.

Institute of Management Consultants USA (IMC USA)
631 US Highway 1, Suite 400
North Palm Beach, FL 33408
website: www.imcusa.org

IMC USA provides certification for management consultants. It also puts on national conferences and provides numerous online resources.

National Management Association (NMA)
2210 Arbor Blvd.
Dayton, OH 45439
website: https://nma1.org

The NMA is a professional association dedicated to developing leadership and management skills. It offers certification and continuing education units to members.

Society of Professional Consultants
3 Stonebolt Way
Westford, MA 01886
website: www.spconsultants.org

This organization represents consultants. It strives to help them grow their businesses and provide the best service to their clients. The organization's website provides links to resources, mentoring services, newsletters, and other information.

Marketing Manager

What Does a Marketing Manager Do?

Marketing managers ensure that organizations meet their sales goals. They conduct research and evaluate demand for a company's products (that is, how many people want to buy which product or service). They oversee the creation of plans to increase demand for products and help identify potential new markets or audiences. They pinpoint a company's target audience—that is, who a company should be selling its products to—and figure out the best way to reach that audience. Marketing managers also help determine what to charge for a company's products and services—such prices need to be both profitable and competitive. Marketing managers also build a company's brand awareness using e-mail campaigns, newsletters, contests, and celebrity endorsements and by placing products in television shows and movies. They often work closely with the company's sales department, public relations team, and product development staff.

The role of the marketing manager can vary by organization. In a large, multinational company

---

At a Glance
Marketing Manager

Minimum Educational Requirements
Bachelor's degree

Personal Qualities
Strong communication and interpersonal skills; creativity

Certification and Licensing
Not required, but can strengthen résumé

Working Conditions
Office environment

Salary Range
Median pay of $128,750 in 2015

Number of Jobs
As of 2014, about 194,300

Future Job Outlook
Projected increase of 9 percent through 2024

A marketing manager reviews sales figures and other information as part of compiling a monthly report. The job of the marketing manager is to ensure that a company meets its sales goals.

a marketing manager may be responsible for developing and maintaining a brand's image. In a smaller company a marketing manager may help introduce new products to the market and provide marketing support. He or she might be responsible for several services or products or just one.

Marketing managers work with the sales department and other team members to come up with ideas for advertising campaigns. They may be involved in designing a product's packaging. They may also decide which media outlets to advertise on, such as television, radio, Internet, newspapers, or outdoor signs. In larger companies marketing managers often oversee an in-house team that creates the advertising. They may also be involved in hiring and supervising creative staff, negotiating ad contracts, and approving ad designs. They work with the finance department to create and monitor the ad campaign's budget.

In some situations a company may outsource its advertising campaign to an advertising or promotion agency. In this case the marketing manager often serves as the liaison between the company and the advertising agency.

Marketing managers also monitor the market. They measure customer demand for a company's products and services, as well as demand for a competitor's products. They watch market trends to identify when a new product might be needed. Once the company comes up with an idea for a new product, marketing managers work closely with other departments—such as engineering or product design—to develop it. Along with the sales and public relations departments, marketing managers monitor how satisfied customers are with the company's products and quickly address any issues involving those who are unsatisfied.

Daniel Helmhold is the director of product marketing for Kabam, an entertainment company that makes games for mobile devices. In a July 2012 interview on the Bloomberg website, Helmhold described a project he worked on as the company's global produce marketing manager, in which he created a publication that showcased the main reasons a customer should buy a particular product. "It might include screen shots, a bit about the story, a blurb about what is so successful and special; it could be used for a cover letter or a press release, or be brought to a media event, conference, or recruiting event," he said. He also works on projects to cross-promote games, which involves getting people who like to play one game to play another one of the company's games.

How Do You Become a Marketing Manager?

Education

Most marketing managers have at least a bachelor's degree from a four-year college or university. They typically major in business administration, marketing, or a related field. Some employers prefer candidates to have a master's degree in business administration. Students interested in this field should take classes in marketing, consumer behavior, market research, sales, visual arts, and communication methods and technology. Courses in business law, management, economics, finance, computer science, mathematics, and statistics are also helpful. For example, a computer science course might help a marketing manager improve a company's website traffic and use digital promotions.

Many marketing managers continue to educate themselves long after they have finished school. They take continuing education classes and read current industry research papers. They also keep up-to-date on the latest technologies and learn how to use new software and social media platforms.

Many marketing managers have several years of related work experience. They may have worked as a sales representative, advertising specialist, buyer or purchasing agent, or in public relations. These positions offer valuable experience that translates well to being a marketing manager. For example, working in sales helps someone learn to interact with customers and determine consumer needs, both of which are critical for being a marketing manager.

Certification and Licensing

Although marketing managers do not need any special licenses, choosing to undergo training or get certifications can improve their chances of landing a job or being promoted. Taking certification courses, training seminars, and courses organized by professional societies and universities can show that a person is committed to improving his or her knowledge and skills. Marketing managers also attend local and national conferences to stay on top of the latest industry trends. Some also join professional organizations such as the American Marketing Association, which provides networking opportunities and hosts job boards and seminars.

Volunteer Work and Internships

Many marketing managers do an internship while they are in college or graduate school. One is Dean Rice, who in 2015 worked a four-month internship with Red Chair Communications, a marketing and communications agency that works with nonprofit organizations. While interning, Rice worked on a variety of projects that included writing a script for a video and presenting a new business opportunity to senior management. Rice says the internship allowed him to learn new skills in a real-life setting. "If each project you are assigned is not somewhat challenging, what's the point?" he said in a 2015 interview published on the Association Headquarters website. "All young professionals alike need to get out of their comfort zone initially to truthfully find out what work suits them best."

Skills and Personality

Successful marketing managers have strong interpersonal, communication, and analytical skills. Marketing managers spend a lot of their time working with other team members and customers. This makes it important to have strong interpersonal skills and to work well with people of all backgrounds. Marketing managers also need to be strong leaders, since part of their job involves motivating employees and other team members to do their best.

Marketing managers must also have strong communication and presentation skills. Part of their job involves understanding clients' or customers' needs; this involves having good listening skills and paying attention to detail. They must understand those needs so well that they are able to explain them to those whose job it is to design or sell products. They need to be analytical and have good decision-making skills—this helps them choose the right media for an advertising campaign, for example. Developing advertising and promotional strategies also takes a lot of creativity. At the same time, planning and directing multiple campaigns requires strict organizational and time-management skills.

Marketing managers must also have up-to-date computer skills. They should be comfortable using basic word processing and database programs. Having solid Internet skills and understanding social media platforms can help them perform Internet marketing and research.

On the Job

Employers and Working Conditions

Marketing managers work in virtually every industry. While some work directly for large organizations, others work for consulting firms that contract with other companies on special projects. Others are self-employed and work on a project-by-project basis. According

52

to the Bureau of Labor Statistics (BLS), there were approximately 194,300 marketing managers working in 2014. The industries that employed the most marketing managers were professional, scientific, and technical services (21 percent); manufacturing (12 percent); finance and insurance (10 percent); and wholesale trade (9 percent). In addition, approximately 17 percent of marketing managers were hired by company management.

Because their work directly affects a company's revenue and profits, marketing managers often work closely with a company's top executives. The job can be stressful, because they are often under intense pressure to meet targets, goals, and deadlines. As a result, marketing managers often work long hours or on weekends.

Most of the time, marketing managers work in an office. They often travel to attend trade shows or meet with clients and media representatives such as video production companies and print production companies.

Earnings

According to the BLS, as of May 2015 the median annual earnings for marketing managers was $128,750. Because marketing managers' duties vary by industry and organization, earnings also vary. In 2014 wages ranged from less than $66,090 to more than $187,200 for the highest-paid managers.

In addition, marketing managers who work for an organization or consulting firm typically receive other benefits, which can amount to thousands of dollars. Benefits vary from employer to employer. These benefits can include paid vacation and sick leave, bonuses, medical and dental insurance, education benefits and tuition reimbursement, retirement benefits, and life insurance.

Opportunities for Advancement

Experienced marketing managers usually get to take on more responsibility and work on complex projects. Senior managers may supervise teams of employees on a large project. Some marketing managers may advance to higher-level positions, such as director of marketing. Some may even become a top executive in their firm. Others might leave an organization and start their own consulting company.

Experienced marketing managers with a track record of excellent work are more likely to be considered for a promotion. In addition, those who have earned professional certifications or a master's degree in business administration are also more likely to have more opportunities to advance.

What Is the Future Outlook for Marketing Managers?

The job outlook for marketing managers is very good. According to the BLS's *Occupational Outlook Handbook*, marketing manager jobs are projected to grow 9 percent from 2014 to 2024. This rate of growth is faster than the average for all occupations.

As organizations try to maintain and grow their market share, they will need to conduct advertising, promotional, and marketing campaigns. Therefore, they will need marketing managers to plan, direct, and coordinate such campaigns. As more and more customers use the Internet, managers who have the skills to conduct digital media campaigns (via websites, social media, or live chats) will be especially in demand.

In some cases improving technology may limit employment opportunities in this field. The Internet allows marketing managers to reach a larger target audience across many platforms. In addition, better advertising management software allows managers to more efficiently plan and control campaigns, which may decrease the number of professionals needed to oversee marketing campaigns. However, because marketing managers directly help an organization meet its revenue goals, they are less likely to be laid off than other types of managers.

Marketing managers are generally well paid, which makes these jobs highly desired. Therefore, candidates will face strong competition for open positions. Those who have a graduate degree or certification, have related work experience, or are fluent in a foreign language will have an advantage when searching for a job. In addition, as more companies rely on Internet-based marketing, managers who have digital skills and experience will have access to the best opportunities.

Find Out More

American Marketing Association (AMA)
130 E. Randolph St., 22nd Floor
Chicago, IL 60601
website: www.ama.org

The AMA's website features a Student Resource Center that has information and resources to help people who are considering a career in marketing.

Business Marketing Association
708 Third Ave.
New York, NY 10017
website: www.marketing.org

The Business Marketing Association focuses on business-to-business marketing. It provides information, case studies, and other information on its website.

Careers-in-Marketing
website: www.careers-in-marketing.com

This website offers a lot of information about different careers in marketing, including advertising, market research, retail, and product management, along with links to other marketing career sites.

Internet Marketing Association
website: http://imanetwork.org

The Internet Marketing Association is dedicated to creating standards for the Internet marketing industry. Its website provides information and resources for people interested in this field.

Sales Manager

What Does a Sales Manager Do?

Sales managers direct a company's sales team. They supervise a team of sales representatives, set sales goals for individual representatives, and assign representatives sales territories (areas in which they operate). They also recruit, hire, mentor, and train new sales representatives. Large organizations may have several levels of sales managers; higher-level managers tend to oversee whole regions and local sales managers.

Sales managers also analyze sales statistics to determine how much inventory a company should have on hand to fill future orders and track customer preferences. Based on their analysis, they estimate how many products the company will sell in a certain period and calculate how much money a company's products and services will make. They use their estimates to prepare budgets for the sales department and help senior management estimate how much revenue the company can expect to earn for a certain period.

At a Glance
Sales Manager

Minimum Educational Requirements
Bachelor's degree

Personal Qualities
Strong leadership, communication, and analytical skills

Certification and Licensing
Not required, but can strengthen résumé

Working Conditions
Office environment

Salary Range
Median pay of $113,860 in 2015

Number of Jobs
As of 2014, about 376,300

Future Job Outlook
Projected increase of 5 percent through 2024

Sales managers work closely with an organization's other departments. For example, the marketing department may do research that generates leads for new customers; it will give these leads to the sales department so it knows whom to target. Sales managers also work closely with warehouse and design staff. Because members of the sales team deal directly with clients, they can communicate customer needs to the design team and inventory needs to the warehouse staff.

Some sales managers specialize in business-to-business (B2B) sales. B2B sales are when one company sells to another company instead of to a retail consumer. For example, a sales manager may work for a manufacturer like Nike and sell shoes and clothing to a retail company like Dick's Sporting Goods. Other sales managers specialize in business-to-consumer (B2C) sales. An example of a B2C business is Toys"R"Us, which sells toys and other products directly to consumers. These managers often work for retail companies such as car dealerships, sporting goods stores, and grocery stores.

Damien Swendsen is a sales manager at a large West Coast tech company. He likes the variety that every day brings to his job. In an April 2013 interview on the AfterCollege website, he said:

> You never know what you're going to do. . . . You might be up at 6 a.m. for a call with the East Coast, spend some time returning emails or calls, have sales meetings (with a client or prospect, giving demonstrations, finding out their needs), and attend internal meetings (pipeline meetings, review with boss, discussions with different sides like marketing and service support). And on that same day you might have a golf meeting or a two-hour lunch to build relationships and then a 9 p.m. call with Singapore.

Swendsen said that one of the best parts of his job is the flexibility and compensation, but he admitted there can be some drawbacks. "If you're not producing, you won't get paid," he said. "There's the stress of meeting the deadlines, and it's harder to get away because you always have email and your phone, so there's less separation between work and life."

How Do You Become a Sales Manager?

Education

Most sales managers have at least a bachelor's degree from a four-year college or university. They likely majored in business administration, marketing, or a related field. Some employers prefer candidates to have a master's degree in business administration. Students interested in this career should take classes in business law, management, economics, accounting, finance, mathematics, marketing, and statistics.

Most employers require sales managers to have at least one to five years' prior work experience in sales. Students interested in becoming a sales manager can start their career by working as a sales representative or a purchasing agent.

Certification and Licensing

Although sales managers do not need any specific certifications or licenses to do their work, some get additional training and/or earn a certification such as the Certified Professional Salesperson offered by Sales and Marketing Executives International. This additional work demonstrates that individuals are committed to learning more and updating their skills. Sales managers also attend local and national conferences to stay on top of the latest trends in the industry. Topics often include product promotion, marketing communication, sales management evaluation, direct sales, and brand and product management.

Volunteer Work and Internships

Students interested in this field might consider doing a sales internship. In April 2015 Dijana Druskic worked as a sales and marketing intern for Inchoo, a software company. During her four weeks with the company, Druskic says she learned a lot about sales. "I became more aware of how sales actually works," she said in a 2015 interview published on the Inchoo website. "I saw how teams function when their productivity has the priority, and their willingness to go an extra mile for their clients."

Skills and Personality

Successful sales managers are good motivators and mentors, with strong communication skills. They collect and analyze complex sales data, such as the amount and types of products or services sold and the number, types, and locations of customers. They then use that information to determine the company's sales strategies and deploy sales staff and resources. As leaders of a sales team, they must motivate and mentor sales representatives and position them to meet personal and company goals. "As a new sales manager, coaching is one of the most important skills you need to master to drive sales performance," said Norman Behar, chief executive officer and managing director of Sales Readiness Group. In a 2013 article on the Heinz Marketing website, he said, "Great coaches empower their teams to achieve their full potential. This involves actively listening, coaching to promote self-discovery, and inspiring their teams."

Because sales managers spend a lot of time interacting with customers, sales representatives, and other department managers, they must communicate clearly and effectively, both in written reports and oral presentations. When making a sale, sales managers must demonstrate good listening skills so they can respond to a customer's needs.

As more work is completed digitally and over the Internet, it is increasingly important for sales managers to have top-notch computer skills. Also, sales managers sometimes work in regions where customers do not speak English. It is thus helpful to be able to communicate in a foreign language.

On the Job

Employers and Working Conditions

Sales managers work in many industries. According to the Bureau of Labor Statistics (BLS), there were approximately 376,300 sales managers working in 2014. The industries that employed the most sales managers in 2014 were retail trade (20 percent); wholesale trade (20 percent); manufacturing (12 percent); finance and insurance (9 percent); and professional, scientific, and technical services (8 percent).

Most sales managers work full time, and many work some evenings and weekends. Because they are often under intense pressure to meet sales targets, their job can be stressful. "The constant push for higher and higher numbers and the expectations behind the job are very stressful," said Connie Larson, a sales manager for a Black House White Market retail store in California, in a 2013 article published on the Women's eNews website. In addition, it can require a significant amount of travel to meet with customers, dealers, distributors, and other industry professionals. Sales managers are also expected to travel to regional or national company offices to attend meetings and other functions.

Earnings

According to the BLS, as of May 2015 the median annual earnings for sales managers was $113,860. A sales manager's compensation plan varies by company. Most plans feature a combination of salary plus commissions and bonuses. Commissions are generally calculated as a percentage of sales, while bonuses can be tied to an individual's performance, the performance of all sales staff in a region, or the entire organization's performance. In 2014 wages for sales managers ranged from less than $54,490 to more than $187,200 for the highest-paid managers.

In addition, sales managers typically receive other benefits, which can amount to thousands of dollars. Benefits vary from employer to employer and include paid vacation and sick leave, medical and dental insurance, education benefits and tuition reimbursement, retirement benefits, and life insurance.

Opportunities for Advancement

Many sales managers often begin their careers as sales representatives, purchasing agents or buyers, or promotion specialists. Although they may want to move up the ladder quickly, the experience and knowledge they gain at lower levels can make them better managers. Damien Swendsen explains:

> It can be tough the first couple of years. People just want immediate gratification and benefits, but you

have to put the work in and understand things from the bottom up. You have to have that experience of being at the bottom rung and working your way up. It's like a chef—unless you've learned the basics, you won't be able to create a beautiful wedding cake. You need those things that seem a little boring and mundane to build upon and become successful later on.

Sales managers in larger companies with multiple layers of managers have a better chance of being promoted. Senior sales managers may supervise all of the sales managers in a large company. Some may advance to higher-level positions, such as regional sales manager. Some even become top executives in their firm.

Experienced sales managers who have proved themselves have a better chance of being promoted. Those with additional training, such as certifications or a master's degree in business administration, may also be more likely to advance.

What Is the Future Outlook for Sales Managers?

The job outlook for sales managers is good. According to the BLS's *Occupational Outlook Handbook*, employment of sales managers is projected to grow 5 percent from 2014 to 2024. This rate of growth is the same as the average growth for all occupations. The growth rate for these jobs by industry will depend on the overall industry growth rate.

Companies need effective sales teams if they are to meet the company's revenue and profit goals. Talented sales managers are expected to be in demand as organizations look to develop sales strategies to generate new sales and increase their market share. One of the main drivers of growth in this field is expected to come from growth in B2B sales. At the same time, growth in online shopping is expected to decrease the need for B2C sales representatives and managers, because people who shop online do so without the help of a sales rep or manager.

Sales managers are generally well paid, which makes these jobs highly desired. Therefore, candidates will face strong competition for open positions. Candidates who have related work experience, fluency in a foreign language, and demonstrated leadership ability will have an advantage when searching for a job. In addition, as more companies rely on Internet-based sales and marketing, sales managers who have experience and skills in the digital world will have the best opportunities.

Find Out More

American Association of Inside Sales Professionals
1593 112th Court West
Inver Grove Heights, MN 55077
website: www.aa-isp.org

The American Association of Inside Sales Professionals provides information and resources for people in or interested in a career in inside sales (sales by phone or online instead of face-to-face meetings with customers).

National Association of Sales Professionals
website: www.nasp.com

This association provides a sales-only job board, a news stream dedicated to sales-related news, and a library of resources geared toward sales, marketing, and social media. It also features a sales certification area.

Sales Association
2460 W. Twenty-Sixth Ave., Suite 245-C
Denver, CO 80211
website: www.salesassociation.org

The Sales Association is a society for sales professionals in all businesses and industries. The association offers networking and professional development opportunities for sales professionals.

Sales Management Association
website: http://salesmanagement.org

The Sales Management Association is a global, cross-industry professional organization for sales operations and sales management that promotes professional development, peer networking, and research and discussion about successful sales strategies.

Financial Manager

What Does a Financial Manager Do?

Financial managers manage an organization's finances. They oversee several employees and supervise the production of financial reports, budgets, and forecasts (predictions of what might happen regarding the business's financials). Using these reports and other data, financial managers find ways to reduce costs and increase profits. They monitor the company's finances to make sure the company is following laws and regulations. They also direct investment activities and help develop strategies to achieve the organization's long-term financial goals.

Because technology has made it easier and faster to gather financial data and prepare reports, financial managers are increasingly being asked to perform more data analysis and suggest ways to cut costs and maximize profits. Mazhar Mahmood, a commercial finance manager at a British company called Digital Catapult, says he spends a lot of time analyzing financial data and building financial models. Mahmood says that

At a Glance

Financial Manager

Minimum Educational Requirements

Bachelor's degree; master's degree preferred

Personal Qualities

Strong communication, analytical, math, and financial skills

Certification and Licensing

Not required, but can strengthen résumé

Working Conditions

Office environment

Salary Range

Median pay of $117,990 in 2015

Number of Jobs

As of 2014, about 555,900

Future Job Outlook

Projected growth of 7 percent through 2024

he often works as part of a team with people from several different departments, providing finance data as needed.

The job of a financial manager varies by organization and by industry. For example, a financial manager for a health care provider must know about health care regulations and insurance reimbursements. A financial manager for a software company, on the other hand, must be aware of industry-specific accounting and revenue recognition rules. He or she must know about tax laws and regulations that affect his or her particular industry and organization.

Chief financial officers (CFOs), controllers, and treasurers are types of high-level financial managers. CFOs head an organization's financial department. They supervise lower-level financial managers and oversee the organization's financial goals and budgets. In a publicly traded company, the CFO must make sure a company's financial reports are accurate. Controllers generally report to the CFO and direct finance staff to prepare financial reports. These include income statements, balance sheets, cash flow reports, budgets, and forecasts. Controllers also manage the preparation of any required regulatory or tax reports. Treasurers oversee investments and are responsible for developing strategies to raise capital for the company, such as issuing stocks or bonds. They are also involved in financial planning for mergers and acquisitions.

Lower-level financial managers include credit managers, cash managers, risk managers, and insurance managers. These managers oversee a small team of employees and focus on a specific area of finance. For example, credit managers oversee an organization's accounts payable department and monitor the collection of past-due accounts. They decide how to classify customers at different risk levels for credit and set limits on the amount of credit the company gives a customer.

Steffanie Dorn is the finance director for the town of Greenwood, South Carolina. She spends most of her time reviewing the entries in the accounting system, preparing reports, and providing information for the city manager and city council. She also oversees the production of financial statements, accounts payable, payroll, and revenue collections. She says that technology has changed the way she does her job. "When I started, the Internet was really in its infancy and was not something that I used daily. Now, I check our bank balance every day on the Internet and often use it for other purposes," Dorn said in a 2013 interview on the Municipal Association of South Carolina website. Dorn said her office is using technology to become paperless and more efficient. For example, the staff scans paid invoices instead of filing them and e-mails documents when possible. "We send a lot of documents via email rather than copying and snail mailing," Dorn said. "Recently, we began emailing deposit slips to employees rather than printing on paper and are implementing email of business license renewals and sanitation bills."

How Do You Become a Finance Manager?

Education

Most finance managers have at least a bachelor's degree in finance, accounting, economics, or business administration. Many employers prefer candidates who have a master's degree in business administration, finance, or economics. These programs teach students financial analysis and help them develop the analytical skills they will need for a career in finance.

Employers also prefer candidates who have work experience in a business or financial occupation. Finance managers can gain this experience by working as a loan officer, accountant, securities sales agent, or financial analyst. In some cases large companies provide formal management training to help talented financial workers become finance managers.

Certification and Licensing

Financial managers do not need to be certified to do their job. However, obtaining a certification can demonstrate competence and skill. Professional organizations such as the CFA Institute and the Association for Financial Professionals offer several certifications that can strengthen a candidate's résumé. The education, experience, and testing requirements vary for each certification.

Some financial managers who work as accountants choose to become certified public accountants (CPAs) or certified management accountants. Investment professionals may choose to obtain the

Chartered Financial Analyst certification, while those who work in treasury departments may choose to pursue a Certified Treasury Professional credential.

Most financial professionals attend continuing education classes to keep up with the latest finance and accounting industry news. These classes help them understand changes in federal and state laws, new financial innovations, and global trade and accounting policies. Many organizations will pay for part or all of the cost of attending such classes.

Volunteer Work and Internships

Students interested in this career are advised to volunteer for local companies and nonprofit organizations. They can also shadow an employee who works in this field or do an internship. For example, during the summer of 2014, Andrew Kennedy, a finance major at Elon University in North Carolina, worked as a corporate finance intern at Bain Capital in Boston. He audited employee time and expense reports, processed checks for employee expense reimbursements, and entered invoices into the company's software accounting program. In an interview published on the Elon University website, Kennedy said that his internship "was a great opportunity to learn the ins and outs of the business and give me more experience to go along with my degree. I wanted to take what I have learned in class to real life and put it to use."

Skills and Personality

Successful finance managers need good analytical, math, and computer skills. Because they prepare and analyze financial reports for top executives, they need solid math skills to understand complex finance topics. Financial managers are also often asked to analyze data and help senior management make decisions and establish strategy. They must therefore be very analytical and be able to make solid decisions. Strong communication skills are also essential, since financial managers often need to explain complex financial information to other managers and executives in the organization. Because they work with numerous documents and data systems, finance managers must also be very organized.

Finance managers should also have strong computer skills. They need to be able to use word processing, spreadsheet, and database software. They also need to have experience working with accounting and financial reporting systems.

On the Job

Employers and Working Conditions

Every company needs to generate and interpret financial reports and records. According to the Bureau of Labor Statistics (BLS), there were approximately 555,900 finance managers working in 2014. The industries that employed the most finance managers were finance and insurance (29 percent); professional, scientific, and technical services (11 percent); manufacturing (8 percent); and government (7 percent). In addition, about 12 percent of finance managers were hired as consultants.

Regardless of industry, most finance managers work in an office. They often work closely with top executives. Most finance managers work full time, or forty hours per week. Overtime is sometimes necessary, particularly when deadlines for filing financial reports and other paperwork are near. In 2014 approximately one-third of finance managers worked more than forty hours per week.

Earnings

According to the BLS, as of May 2015 the median annual earnings for finance managers was $117,990. The lowest 10 percent earned less than $63,020, while the highest 10 percent earned more than $187,200.

In addition, finance managers typically receive other benefits, which can include paid vacation and sick leave, bonuses, medical and dental insurance, education benefits, retirement benefits, and life insurance. These benefits vary from employer to employer and can amount to thousands of dollars.

Opportunities for Advancement

Finance managers who work for larger organizations generally have more opportunities to advance to higher positions. They typically start in entry-level positions and move up to become managers, positions that have additional responsibility. Others advance to higher-level positions, such as CFO, controller, or treasurer.

Experienced finance managers who demonstrate a thorough knowledge of their organization, its needs, and its regulatory requirements are more likely to be promoted. Professionals who earn certifications or a master's degree in business administration may be more likely to be considered for a promotion.

What Is the Future Outlook for Finance Managers?

According to the BLS's *Occupational Outlook Handbook*, finance manager jobs are projected to increase 7 percent from 2014 to 2024. This rate of growth is about the same as the average growth rate for all occupations.

As the economy grows, financial managers will continue to be in demand. As companies accumulate cash assets, they will need financial managers who have experience handling and investing cash to plan, direct, and coordinate investments. The increasing use of technology may have a negative effect on the number of jobs for financial staff, since fewer people will be needed to perform the same amount of work. However, this is expected to have a greater impact on lower-level finance staff, since technology will allow companies to use fewer people to manage and process financial transactions and records. The need for finance managers who can analyze data and recommend how to improve company profits is expected to continue, because this type of analysis is an important part of helping a company succeed. "Finance jobs are quickly becoming some of the most senior, impactful roles within commercial businesses," says Thomas Winters, a commercial finance manager at Uniting Ambition, a UK recruiting firm, in an interview on the firm's website.

Overall, finance managers have good job prospects. Although competition for jobs will be intense, candidates who have experience in accounting and finance and have a master's degree or certification will have the best prospects. In addition, as more companies enter the global marketplace, candidates who understand international finance and complex documents (such as financial statements and tax returns) will have an advantage.

Find Out More

American Institute of Certified Public Accountants (AICPA)
1211 Avenue of the Americas
New York, NY 10036
website: www.aicpa.org

The AICPA represents the CPA profession nationally. Its website provides information and resources for people interested in obtaining a CPA certification and working as a CPA. It also posts industry research, publications, and CPA-related news.

Association for Financial Professionals (AFP)
4520 E. West Hwy., Suite 800
Bethesda, MD 20814
website: www.afponline.org

The AFP is the professional society that represents finance executives globally. The AFP established and administers the Certified Treasury Professional and Certified Corporate FP&A Professional credentials.

CFA Institute
website: www.cfainstitute.org

The CFA Institute sets professional standards for investment management practitioners and develops future professionals through its credentialing programs.

Financial Management Association International (FMA)
University of South Florida
College of Business Administration
4202 E. Fowler Ave., BSN 3416
Tampa, FL 33620
website: www.fma.org

A nonprofit organization, the FMA publishes research on important financial issues, hosts annual finance conferences, and brings together professionals who share a common interest in finance.

Interview with a Human Resources Manager

Melissa Malloy is a human resources manager at KPMG, an accounting firm in Pittsburgh, Pennsylvania. She has worked for four years in her current position. She answered questions about her career by e-mail.

Q: Why did you decide to work in this career?

A: Because it gave me the opportunity to combine my love of accounting (as nerdy as that sounds) with my love of the people side of business. It also allows me to continue to grow and become well-rounded in the business world. I'm a CPA [certified public accountant] who worked in public accounting, took an opportunity to work in finance at a growing manufacturing company, and then decided to return to the people side of things, acting as campus recruiter and resource manager. I most recently moved into a fully-focused regional HR role.

I've loved each step along the way. I was able to gain valuable experience with each role—accounting, finance, logistics/planning, and now all things people-related. I feel as though I'm successful in my current role because of my diverse background, which gives me a true sense of the issues that employees are facing—I've been in their shoes before. The greatest feeling is helping other people while helping a business be successful.

Q: Can you describe your typical workday?

A: In today's business world there really is no typical workday! My days usually involve several meetings or calls, as I work with a lot of people who are in different locations. Thanks to technology, collaboration is fairly easy regardless of how far away the collaborators are. I deal with things related to employee morale, performance management, compensation, ethics and compliance, legal issues, medical issues, immigration, and any other personnel issues (this can run a spectrum of things).

Q: What do you like most about your job?
A: The thing I love the most is helping people—whether it's helping students find the right fit with their first job at the firm, or helping current employees with difficult situations. If I can make someone's life better in some way, I feel great about that.

Q: What do you like least about your job?
A: The thing I like the least about my job is having the difficult conversations, most notably when we have to let someone go from the firm. Regardless of how many times you do it, that part never gets any easier.

Q: What personal qualities do you find most valuable for this type of work?
A: I think a strong work ethic is key in any role you have, but also an understanding of the business and being able to relate to people are key qualities. You need to be able to put yourself in someone else's shoes and see a situation from their perspective—and then tailor your communication to get through to them in a way they will understand.

Q: What advice do you have for students who might be interested in this career?
A: Work hard and do some research to find out what it is you would like about human resources. Make sure you take business communications, presentation, and writing classes and get as much exposure to public speaking as you can. That is extremely helpful in recruiting and human resources (and honestly, business in general). I also think it helps to have a well-rounded skill set—take classes in accounting, finance, marketing, as well as human resources. This will make it easier for you to understand different types of businesses as well as the human resources aspect of the business.

Q: What are the benefits of an internship for students? What advice do you have for someone considering doing one?

A: I've worked a lot with interns in my career and I actually had several internships myself when I was in school. I highly recommend internships for any student—they are a great way to take a job for a test drive before you have to fully commit. In an internship, you get to experience firsthand what you would be doing in a particular job or at a certain company. After the internship, you either decide that you enjoyed it and would like to work in that career, or you decide you didn't like it as much as you thought and now you know it's something you don't want to pursue. Either way, it was a useful tool to get you one step closer to where you truly want to be in life. Internships are a great way for an employer to take you for a test drive as well—if you do a great job, it usually leads to a job offer. In my opinion, internships are definitely beneficial to both students and employers. They're a win-win!

Internships are not easy to land, so I recommend doing some homework and figuring out which companies you would like to target for internships and in what types of industries. Reach out to make connections in advance. Go to career fairs and networking events at school; this is a great way to connect with recruiters and employees. Also, don't count out any opportunity just because it's not exactly what you were looking for. Any experience is good experience—and it may just open new doors that lead to great things!

Other Jobs in Business Administration

Accountant
Account manager
Accounts payable professional
Accounts receivable clerk
Acquisitions tax manager
Agency underwriter
Appraiser
Bank compliance officer
Banker
Benefits and compensation
 manager
Billing clerk
Bookkeeper
Brokerage clerk/assistant
Budget analyst
Business plan writer
Certified personal financial
 planner
Chief lending officer
Claims adjuster
Commercial lender
Commercial loan officer

Construction administrator
Contract negotiator
Corporate auditor
Corporate development
 manager
Corporate travel manager
Credit analyst
Credit counselor
Credit manager
Demand forecast manager
Economist
Escrow closer
Financial analyst
Financial center manager
Forecast analyst
Fund-raiser
Insurance underwriter
Market research analyst
Personal financial advisor
Training and development
 specialist

Editor's Note: The US Department of Labor's Bureau of Labor Statistics provides information about hundreds of occupations. The agency's *Occupational Outlook Handbook* describes what these jobs entail, the work environment, education and skill requirements, pay, future outlook, and more. The *Occupational Outlook Handbook* may be accessed online at www.bls.gov/ooh.

Index

Picture Credits

About the Author

Carla Mooney is the author of many books for young adults and children. She lives in Pittsburgh, Pennsylvania, with her husband and three children.